We—Miranda McPhee and Suzanne Lifson—first met in Paris in 1990.

We have both been traveling since we were very young, and between us we have globetrotted to 35 different countries. We would like to say a huge thanks to our families and friends who helped create this book and gave us ideas, feedback, and encouragement. We made every effort to make sure the content of this activity book is accurate.

Visit us at www.wikidly.com

Contents

How To Use This Book

Bonjour! This WiKIDly Awesome Travels activity book puts you in the middle of Paris, the capital of France. It's an amazing city to visit and with this book you get to participate in the fun in many different ways.

Before your trip, look at all of the neat places you can go to, such as the Eiffel Tower, Notre-Dame Cathedral, the Louvre museum, and marvelous playgrounds. And try out the French words so you can order ice cream!

Here's what you can do every day when you are in Paris: over breakfast, look through your book and talk about what you are going to explore that day. While out and about, test yourself with the quizzes, learn some funky facts you can share with your family and friends, and draw like an artist. Before bed each night, you can think about where you've been, finish your drawings, and dream about the next day's adventures. End your trip by filling in your own Paris story.

This is *your* adventure kids, so have fun!

Bon Voyage!

TRAVEL GUIDE

Travel Information

Name of WiKIDly Awesome Traveler
_____

Date my WiKIDly Awesome Travels to London began   Paris
_____

The people I am traveling with
myMom
_____

Number of days we are spending in London   Paris
_____

Number of miles between my hometown and London   Paris
_____

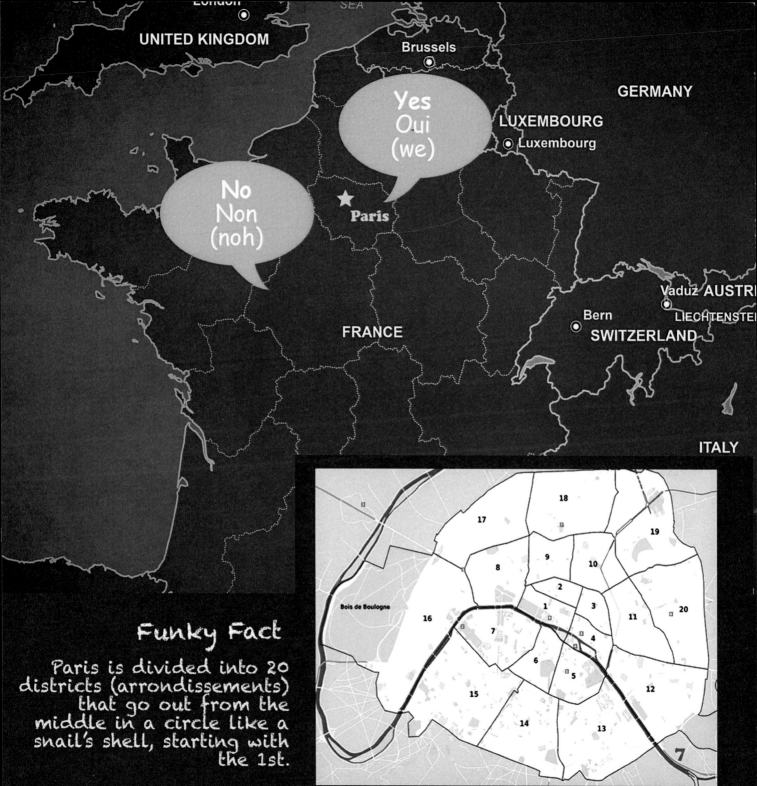

Funky Fact

Paris is divided into 20 districts (arrondissements) that go out from the middle in a circle like a snail's shell, starting with the 1st.

What do you think of Paris so far?

How is the weather?

First Impressions

8

Bonjour, Paris! (bon-joor, paree)

Please
S'il vous plaît
(see voo play)

Thank you
Merci
(mare see)

Quick Quiz

1

What is the Paris subway called?
a) Le train
b) Le métro
c) Le subway

2

What color are mailboxes in Paris?
a) Red
b) Blue
c) Yellow

3

What color are taxi stands?
a) Red
b) Blue
c) Yellow

Funky Fact

There are more than 30 bridges crossing the river Seine.

Memorize the name of the hotel and street where you are staying

9

Learn and practice French phrases and numbers

Speak French!

My name is _____

Je m'appelle _____

(juh ma pell _____)

I am _____ years old

J'ai _____ ans

(jay _____ ahn)

1	2	3	4	5	6
un (uhn)	deux (de)	trois (trwa)	quatre (katre)	cinq (sank)	six (cease)

7	8	9	10	11	12
sept (set)	huit (weet)	neuf (nuff)	dix (dease)	onze (onz)	douze (dooz)

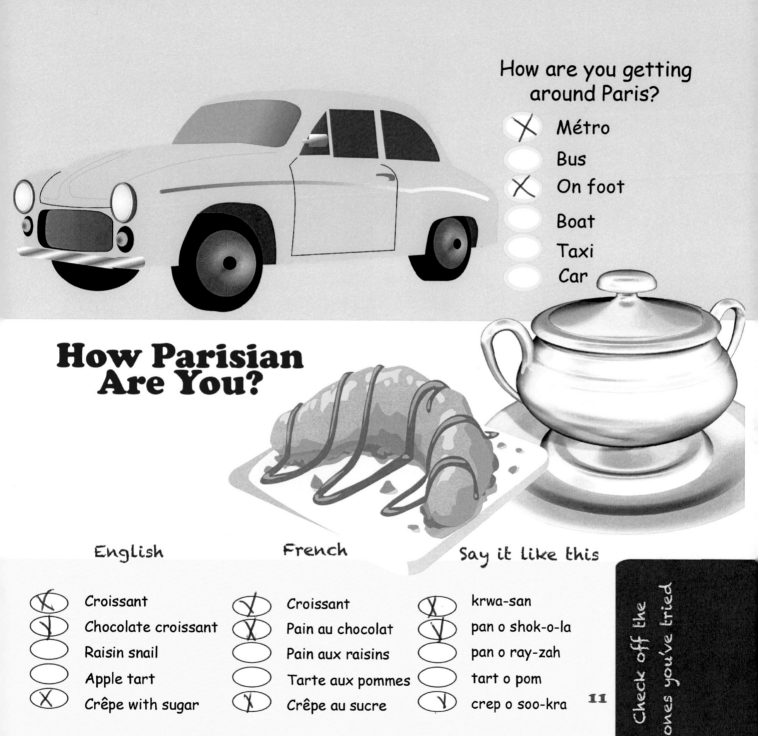

How are you getting around Paris?

- [X] Métro
- [ ] Bus
- [X] On foot
- [ ] Boat
- [ ] Taxi
- [ ] Car

How Parisian Are You?

	English		French		Say it like this
[X]	Croissant	[X]	Croissant	[X]	krwa-san
[X]	Chocolate croissant	[X]	Pain au chocolat	[X]	pan o shok-o-la
[ ]	Raisin snail	[ ]	Pain aux raisins	[ ]	pan o ray-zah
[ ]	Apple tart	[ ]	Tarte aux pommes	[ ]	tart o pom
[X]	Crêpe with sugar	[X]	Crêpe au sucre	[X]	crep o soo-kra

11

Check off the ones you've tried

Funky Fact

The Eiffel Tower was going to be demolished in 1909. Instead, it was kept and used as a giant radio antenna.

History Bits

The Eiffel Tower was built by Gustave Eiffel as a temporary exhibit for the 1889 World Fair. Monsieur Eiffel played a key role in building the Statue of Liberty.

How would you describe the Eiffel Tower to your friends at school?

La Tour Eiffel (la tour F-L)

Draw your own Eiffel Tower here

1

How many light bulbs are on the outside of the Eiffel Tower?

a) 10,000
b) 20,000
c) 30,000

2

How often is the Eiffel Tower painted?

a) Every 7 years
b) Every 8 years
c) Every 11 years

3

How many levels does the Eiffel Tower have?

a) One
b) Two
c) Three

4

How many steps are there between the ground floor and second level?

a) 652
b) 704
c) 946

Funky Fact

At the top of the cathedral are gargoyles -- mythical sculptures with frightening faces.

Check off what you saw.

- [X] Rose windows
- [ ] Great organ
- [X] Gallery of Kings
- [ ] Choir wall
- [ ] Treasury
- [X] Gargoyles

History Bits

The construction of Notre-Dame Cathedral began in 1163 and took more than one hundred years to complete. The cathedral faces east, toward the rising sun, and can hold more than 6,000 people.

The Hunchback of Notre-Dame

This love story was written by French author Victor Hugo. In medieval Paris, Quasimodo is the deformed, hunchbacked bell-ringer of Notre-Dame. He falls in love with Esmeralda, a beautiful gypsy girl who is wrongly accused of murder and is about to be executed. Quasimodo hides her in the cathedral but the peasants think he has kidnapped her, and they come to liberate her.

Notre-Dame de Paris
(no-tra dahm de paree)

Draw your own Notre-Dame here

Quick Quiz

1
What does "Notre-Dame" mean in English?
a) Our Father
b) Big Church
c) Our Lady

2
What is the name of Notre-Dame's biggest bell?
a) Emmanuel
b) Gabriel
c) Marie

3
Notre-Dame sits on which island?
a) Île de la Cité
b) Île de Paris
c) Île de France

Funky Fact

The Louvre subway station is decorated with copies of ancient art from the museum.

History Bits

This museum was originally built as a fortress in 1190. It was then used as a royal palace for hundreds of years before it became a museum in 1793.

1. Find a painting you like. Why do you like it?

2. Who painted it and when?

Le Musée du Louvre
(le mew-zay doo loove)

Draw your favorite piece of art here

Quick Quiz

1

Who painted the Mona Lisa?
a) Rembrandt
b) Da Vinci
c) Monet

2

Venus de Milo represents Aphrodite, the goddess of
a) Love
b) Wisdom
c) Nature

3

What is special about the Galerie d'Apollon?
a) The ceiling
b) The windows
c) The doors

4

What is the pyramid outside the Louvre made of?
a) Stone
b) Marble
c) Glass

The arch is so big that small planes can fly right through the middle of it.

History Bits

In 1806, Emperor Napoleon ordered this arch to be built in honor of his battle victories for France. It is a memorial to all those who have fought for France.

1. What does the Eternal Flame in the middle of the arch symbolize?

2. The location of the arch is called Place de l'Etoile (which means Place of the Star). Why is it called a star?

1._____

_____

2._____

_____

L'Arc de Triomphe
(lark de tree-omph)

Draw your own arch here

Quick Quiz

1
When was the Eternal Flame first lit?
a) 1923
b) 1944
c) 1961

2
What do the names stand for on the 30 shields around the top?
a) Generals
b) Countries
c) Victories

3
What is the Departure of the Volunteers?
a) A statue
b) A sculpture
c) A story

4
Which famous avenue links this arch to the Louvre?
a) Ave. Marceau
b) Les Champs-Elysées
c) Ave. Hoche

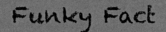

Funky Fact

During the construction, the ground was so wet there was a rumor of a huge fish-filled lake under the building site.

History Bits

This opera house opened in 1875. It is called Palais Garnier (Garnier Palace) after the architect Charles Garnier. You can see both opera and ballet performed here.

1
What are the seven busts (heads) along the front of the building?
a) Emperors
b) Composers
c) Opera singers

2
On top of the building, the figures on the left are called
a) Harmony
b) Destiny
c) Love

3
On top of the building, the figures on the right are called
a) Music
b) Science
c) Poetry

4
The grand staircase was designed for what?
a) Access to seats
b) People-watching
c) A fire escape

The Story of the Phantom of the Opera

In 1910 French author Gaston Leroux used the legend of the lake under the opera house as inspiration for his famous love story, "The Phantom of the Opera." In this story, the Phantom is a man living by the lake. He hides his deformed face behind a mask. He falls in love with Christine, a beautiful and talented opera singer who doesn't love him back. The Phantom kidnaps Christine, hoping to make her fall in love with him.

L'Opéra de Paris

(lopera de paree)

Funky Fact

Before it was a museum, the site was used for many things, including as a movie set for several films.

History Bits

This place was a major railroad terminal from 1900-1939. It stopped being used that way because the new trains were too long for its platforms. It eventually became a museum in 1986.

Fill in the first name of each of these famous artists.

1._____ Cézanne   5._____ Manet   9._____ Sisley

2._____ Degas   6._____ Monet   10._____ Rodin

3._____ Gauguin   7._____ Renoir   11._____ van Gogh

4._____ Pissarro   8._____ Seurat   12._____ Toulouse-Lautrec

Draw the huge clock
inside the museum

1

Outside are three
statues of animals:
a horse, an
elephant, and which
other animal?
a) A rhinoceros
b) A bear
c) A cow

2

In front of the
museum are statues
representing The Six
Continents. What are
the statues of?
a) Trees
b) Women
c) Animals

Quick Quiz

3

Inside the entrance
is a small model of
the Statue of
Liberty. Who
sculpted it?
a) Bartholdi
b) Degas
c) Rodin

4

What is
Impressionism?
a) A language
b) A way to impress
someone
c) A style of
painting

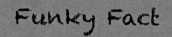

Local people also call this center Beaubourg, which is the name of the area it is in.

History Bits

This colorful cultural and artistic center was designed inside out -- the elevators, escalators, stairways, plumbing, air vents, and electrical cables are on the outside of the building!

Enjoy the colorful art in the museum

See the view from the rooftop

Try the interactive exhibits in the Galerie des Enfants

Ride the external caterpillar escalator in a glass tube

Have fun watching the outside mobiles twist and turn

Le Centre Pompidou
(le son-tr pom-pee-doo)

Draw one of the outdoor exhibits you like

1

When did the Pompidou Centre open?
a) 1968
b) 1977
c) 1998

2

Who was Monsieur Pompidou?
a) A painter
b) A writer
c) A president

Quick Quiz

3

What is in the long tube on the front of the building?
a) An escalator
b) Air conditioning
c) An elevator

4

What is a mobile?
a) A car
b) A work of art that moves in the air
c) An escalator

Funky Fact

The top of the dome is the second-highest lookout point in Paris (the Eiffel Tower is the highest).

History Bits

This basilica stands on a hill called Montmartre, which means "mount of martyrs," originally named after Saint Denis, the Bishop of Paris in 250 A.D.

1
What is the main scene on the front doors?
a) The Last Supper
b) Easter
c) Christmas

2
Where is La Savoyarde (the big bell) located?
a) In the nave
b) In the belfry
c) Outside

3
What is a mosaic made of?
a) Carved wood
b) Small pieces of glass, stone, etc.
c) Paint

4
What do you call the little railway that runs uphill to the church?
a) A funicular
b) A steam train
c) An escalator

Le Sacré-Coeur
(le sack-ray ker)

Place du Tertre

A few streets away from the Sacré-Coeur is a square called La Place du Tertre. Famous artists such as Picasso used to come here to paint. Check out the street artists and watch them draw portraits.

Draw somebody you're traveling with (parent, brother, sister, friend)

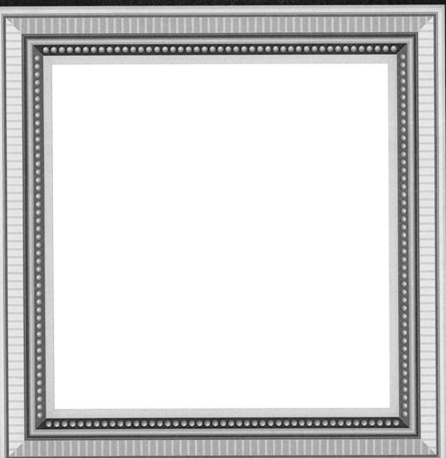

Funky Fact

In 1792 French citizens attacked the Tuileries Palace and overthrew King Louis XVI.

History Bits

The Tuileries Garden, the oldest public park in Paris, first opened to the public in 1667. It gets its name from the tile factories that were here before it became a park ("tuile" means "tile").

Ride the carousel

Have a picnic

Le Jardin des Tuileries
(le jar-duhn day twee-ler-ee)

See a puppet show

You Could...

Sail a small boat

Take the footbridge to the Musée d'Orsay

Feed the ducks

29

Funky Fact

The palace served as a prison during the French Revolution; today, the French Senate meets there.

History Bits

Marie de Medicis, born in Italy, was the wife of King Henry IV of France. She built this palace and garden in 1612 in the style of her hometown in Italy.

Ride on the carousel and be a knight as you try to hook rings on your wooden lance

30

Le Palais et Jardin du Luxembourg
(le pal-ay eh jar-duhn doo loox-em-borg)

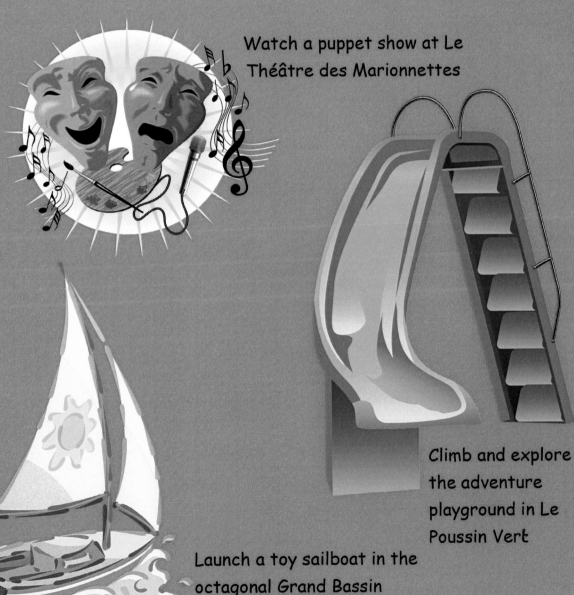

Watch a puppet show at Le Théâtre des Marionnettes

Climb and explore the adventure playground in Le Poussin Vert

Launch a toy sailboat in the octagonal Grand Bassin

31

Funky Fact

This huge, modern park has ten gardens, each of which has a different theme.

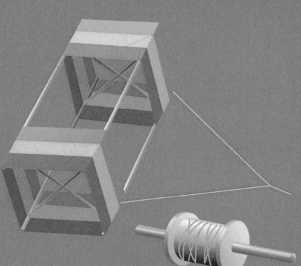

See the kites that look like birds in the Jardin des Equilibres

Visit the planetarium in the Cité des Sciences et de l'Industrie

Parc de la Villette
(park de la vee-let)

Whiz down the slide in the Jardin du Dragon

Check out the pedal windmills in the Jardin des Vents et des Dunes

Check out your reflection in the Jardin des Miroirs

More Paris Adventures

Look out over Paris from the top of the Panthéon dome

Explore Paris by boat with a trip on a Bateau Mouche

See Emperor Napoleon's tomb at Les Invalides

Discover how chocolate is made at the Musée Gourmand du Chocolat

Check out the stained glass windows in La Sainte-Chapelle

The huge, elegant gardens look almost exactly like they did in 1661.

History Bits

Versailles was a royal palace until the French Revolution in 1789. At the end of World War I, the Treaty of Versailles was signed here on June 28, 1919.

1

How many rooms does the palace have?
a) 550
b) 620
c) 700

2

What was Versailles before it was a palace?
a) A hunting lodge
b) A fortress
c) A prison

3

What was the purpose of the Apollo Salon?
a) King's bedroom
b) Throne room
c) Music room

4

What was originally used to light the Hall of Mirrors?
a) Candles
b) Electricity
c) Gas lamps

King Louis XIV - The Sun King
Louis XIV, who lived at Versailles, was crowned king when he was five years old and ruled France for 72 years until he died in 1715. He was known as the Sun King, as he adopted the sun as his emblem (personal symbol). The sun is associated with Apollo, the god of the sun, healing, music, poetry, and more.

Le Palais de Versailles
(Le pa-lay de vair-sigh)

Would you like to live at Versailles? Why or why not?

If you were king or queen, what emblem would you use and why?

Write It Down

37

English

Vanilla
Chocolate
Strawberry
Raspberry
Blackberry
Lemon
Banana
Apricot

French

Vanille
Chocolat
Fraise
Framboise
Cassis
Citron
Banane
Abricot

Say it like this

Van-knee
Shock-oh-la
Frez
Frahm-bwuz
Kass-eece
See-tron
Ba-nan
Ah-bree-co

An ice cream, please

Une glace, s'il vous plaît

Oon glass, see voo play

A crêpe, please

Une crêpe, s'il vous plaît

Oon crep, see voo play

Ice Cream and Crêpes

My Paris Story

Write It Down

What are my favorite Paris memories?

Good bye
Au revoir
(or rev-wha)

Answers to Quick Quizzes

Hello, Paris!	1) b - Le métro 2) c – Yellow 3) b – Blue
Eiffel Tower	1) b – 20,000 2) a – Every 7 years 3) c – Three 4) b – 704
Notre-Dame Cathedral	1) c – Our Lady 2) a – Emmanuel 3) a – Île de la Cité
Louvre Museum	1) b – Da Vinci 2) a - Love 3) a – The ceiling 4) c – Glass
The Arch of Triumph	FIND OUT: 1) The flame burns over the Tomb of the Unknown Soldier in memory of those who gave their lives for France, and is a symbol of hope and faith. 2) 12 avenues stick out from here like the points of a star. QUIZ: 1) a – 1923 2) c – Victories 3) b – A sculpture 4) b – Les Champs-Elysées
Paris Opera	1) b - Composers 2) a - Harmony 3) c - Poetry 4) b – People-watching
D'Orsay Museum	FIND OUT: 1. Paul Cézanne 2. Edgar Degas 3. Paul Gauguin 4. Camille Pissarro 5. Edouard Manet 6. Claude Monet 7. Pierre-Auguste Renoir 8. Georges Seurat 9. Alfred Sisley 10. Auguste Rodin 11. Vincent van Gogh 12. Henri de Toulouse-Lautrec QUIZ: 1) a – A rhinoceros 2) b – Women 3) a – Bartholdi 4) c - A style of painting
Pompidou Center	1) b – 1977 2) c – A president 3) a - An escalator 4) b – A work of art that moves in the air
Basilica of the Sacred Heart	1) a - The Last Supper 2) b – In the belfry 3) b – Small pieces of glass and stone 4) a – A funicular
Versailles	1) c – 700 2) a - A hunting lodge 3) b – Throne room 4) a – Candles

40

21570573R00024

Made in the USA
Middletown, DE
03 July 2015